HOW TO LIVE LIKE...
A VIKING
WARRIOR

Thanks to the creative team:

Senior Editor: Alice Peebles

Designer: Lauren Woods and
collaborate agency

First published in Great Britain in 2015
by Hungry Tomato Ltd

PO Box 181

Edenbridge

Kent, TN8 9DP

A CIP catalogue record for this book is
available from the British Library.

ISBN 978-1-910684-20-7

Printed and bound in China

Discover more at
www.hungrytomato.com

HOW TO LIVE LIKE...
A VIKING WARRIOR

By Anita Ganeri

Illustrated by Mariano Epelbaum

HUNGRY TOMATO™

Being a Viking warrior can be
tiring work. Don't forget to catch
up on sleep whenever you can –
all that fighting and feasting can
take its toll.

Contents

The Viking Warriors

It's the year AD 905. You've travelled back in time to a Viking village on the shores of southern Norway. The long, cold winter is over and everyone's busy getting ready... to go raiding.

Bjorn Sharpaxe at your service, son of the local **jarl** (earl). Rich pickings of gold and treasure from raids have made my father very wealthy. The only person more important is the king (as my Dad's fond of telling everyone). But never mind about all that. The really brilliant news is, now I'm old enough to go raiding this summer with my father and brothers for the first time.

I CANNOT WAIT.

WARNING!

Being a Viking warrior isn't for everyone. You need to be brave and tough. If you don't think you've got what it takes, stick to your farming and stay at home.

Who are the Vikings?

You've ended up in Norway, but Vikings also live in neighbouring Denmark and Sweden. From here, we head off to faraway places in search of plunder, land and trade. Vikings are famous for being fierce warriors and this is true, but we're also brilliant shipbuilders, clever craftsmen and accomplished poets. You'll just have to take my word for it.

Norway

If you're going to be a Viking warrior, you'll need a suitably scary name. Choose something fierce-sounding like Bjorn ('bear'), Ulf ('wolf') or Thorvald, after Thor, the hammer-throwing thunder god.

Training for Raiding

Being a warrior is a top job in Viking society, and it's all I've ever wanted to be. My father gave me my first sword when I was just two years old. It was only wooden, but I still had some good fights with my friends. When I was 10, he gave me my first iron weapons: a sword, a shield and an axe. Since then, I've been training hard every day. My Dad keeps a band of warriors as bodyguards and they've been showing me how to fight. Today's the last day of training before we set off on the raid.

WARNING!

If your father isn't a Jarl, you'll have to work even harder to be picked for a raid. Grab every chance to practise fighting, show willing and you might be in luck.

In our village, you have to be 18 to be picked for a raid. Luckily, I had my birthday last month.

How to keep fit, Viking-style

In between raids, trainee warriors need to keep fit and show fighting spirit. The best way to do this is by being good at sport. Don't pick a sport like football or rugby – they're for wimps. Real Vikings opt for things like wrestling, archery and throwing the javelin (spear).

1 Archery is excellent for developing your hand-eye co-ordination. It's also a handy way of catching something for dinner.

2 Spear-throwing builds upper-body strength and sharpens your competitive edge. After all, you don't want be beaten by Ulf or Thorvald.

3 Wrestling allows you to be aggressive which, for a Viking, is a good thing. If you throw your friends around, you're more likely to be praised than told off.

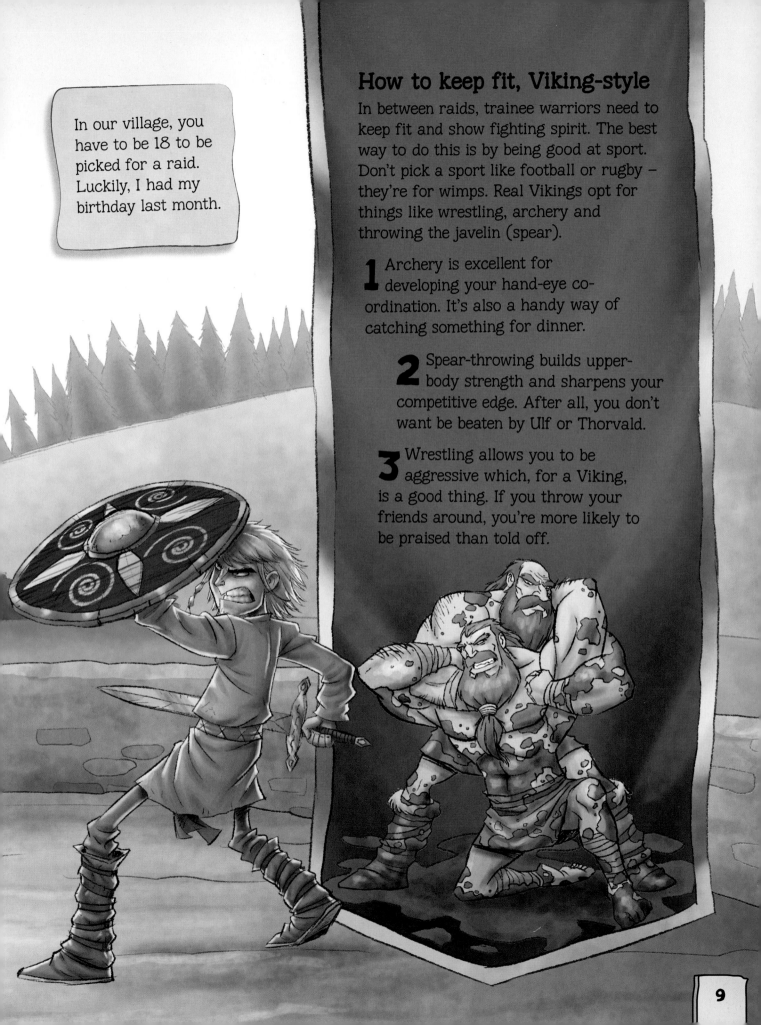

Joining the Hird

Most of the men in our village aren't full-time warriors. They're farmers who join up in summer to sail off on the jarl's raids. If you want to become a professional, you need to join a **hird** (a band of men who fight for a jarl).

As part of the hird, you'll live in the jarl's household, eating and sleeping in his hall. You won't get your own bedroom. You'll have to grab one of the benches by the wall. Try and get as close to the fire as possible.

WARNING!

If you don't like your hird, you can leave without any loss of honour, but you'll have to wait until the New Year.

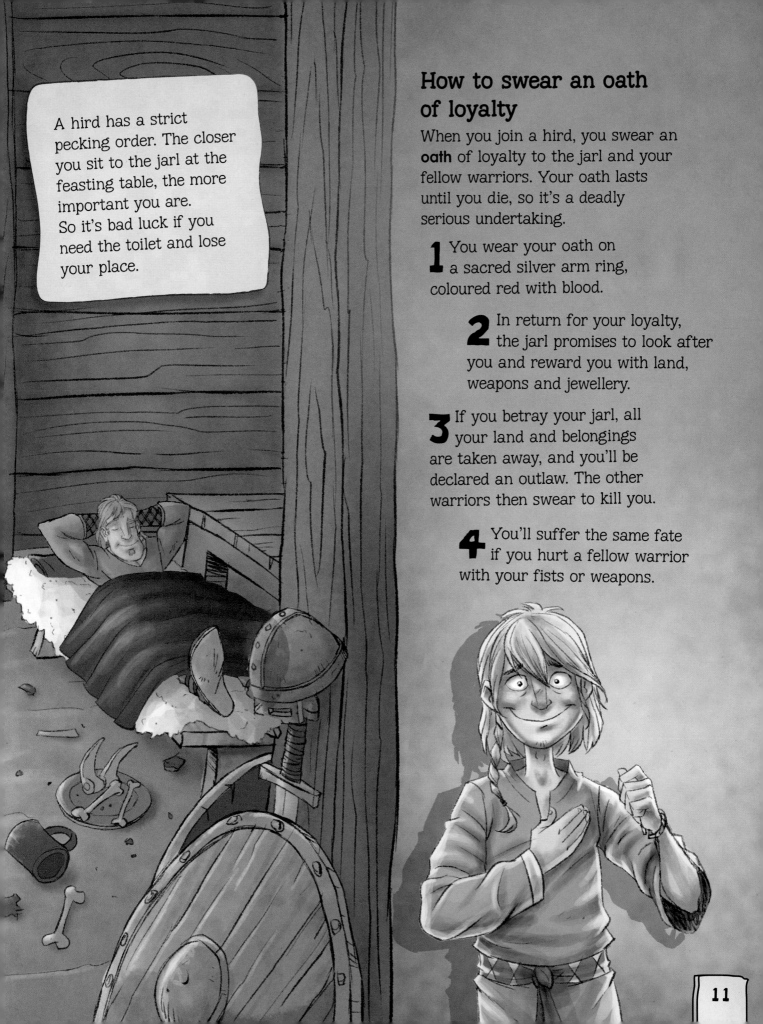

A hird has a strict pecking order. The closer you sit to the jarl at the feasting table, the more important you are.
So it's bad luck if you need the toilet and lose your place.

How to swear an oath of loyalty

When you join a hird, you swear an **oath** of loyalty to the jarl and your fellow warriors. Your oath lasts until you die, so it's a deadly serious undertaking.

1 You wear your oath on a sacred silver arm ring, coloured red with blood.

2 In return for your loyalty, the jarl promises to look after you and reward you with land, weapons and jewellery.

3 If you betray your jarl, all your land and belongings are taken away, and you'll be declared an outlaw. The other warriors then swear to kill you.

4 You'll suffer the same fate if you hurt a fellow warrior with your fists or weapons.

Setting an Example

'You're only as good as your leader,' my father's always saying, and there are plenty of Viking warriors from the past to model yourself on. For years, Dad's told us stories of their cunning, strength and derring-do. Take Erik Bloodaxe....

One of the most famous Vikings ever, brutal Erik Bloodaxe definitely lived up to his bloodthirsty nickname. Leaving a trail of destruction behind, he murdered both of his brothers to make himself King of Norway. Clearly a fearsome warrior, he was also horribly violent and was lucky enough to have clever **skalds** (poets) to big up his dubious deeds.

Ragnar Lodbrok

Young Ragnar Lodbrok ('Hairy-breeches')
fought off his rivals and became King of
Denmark. He then went off raiding until
his luck finally ran out. On his last raid
in England, Ragnar was captured by the
King of Northumbria, and thrown into a
pit of snakes where he was bitten
to death. He died singing about his
exploits. What a guy!

Olaf Tryggvason

Olaf Tryggvason learned about
raiding the hard way. His family
was captured by Vikings in eastern
Europe and he was sold as a slave
in exchange for a cloak. Rescued by
his cousin, he became a top warrior
in the guard of the King of Rus, in
the land that is now Russia. Later,
he raided in Denmark, Sweden and
England. He could even juggle three
knives at a time. He acquired so
much wealth that he was able to
become the King of Norway.

Weapons and Armour

If you want to be a vicious Viking, you need to look the part. The most important bits of a warrior's kit are his weapons so get the best you can afford. Ideally, you'll have a spear, a sword and a battle-axe. There are different spears for stabbing or throwing, and you'll need to master both. There are two kinds of axe, the single-handed axe and the two-handed broad axe. Axes are big and heavy, so give yourself plenty of room to swing. This is when all that fitness training really pays off. Sling your shield over your shoulder while you're swinging, so it protects your back.

What to wear

The best thing to wear into battle is a mail shirt, called a **byrnie.** It's made from thousands of iron rings, welded together. Mail's expensive – my Dad passed his old shirt on to me, but it could save your life. You'll also need a helmet, made of metal or leather, and a shield. Choose one made of wood and leather, with a leather or metal rim.

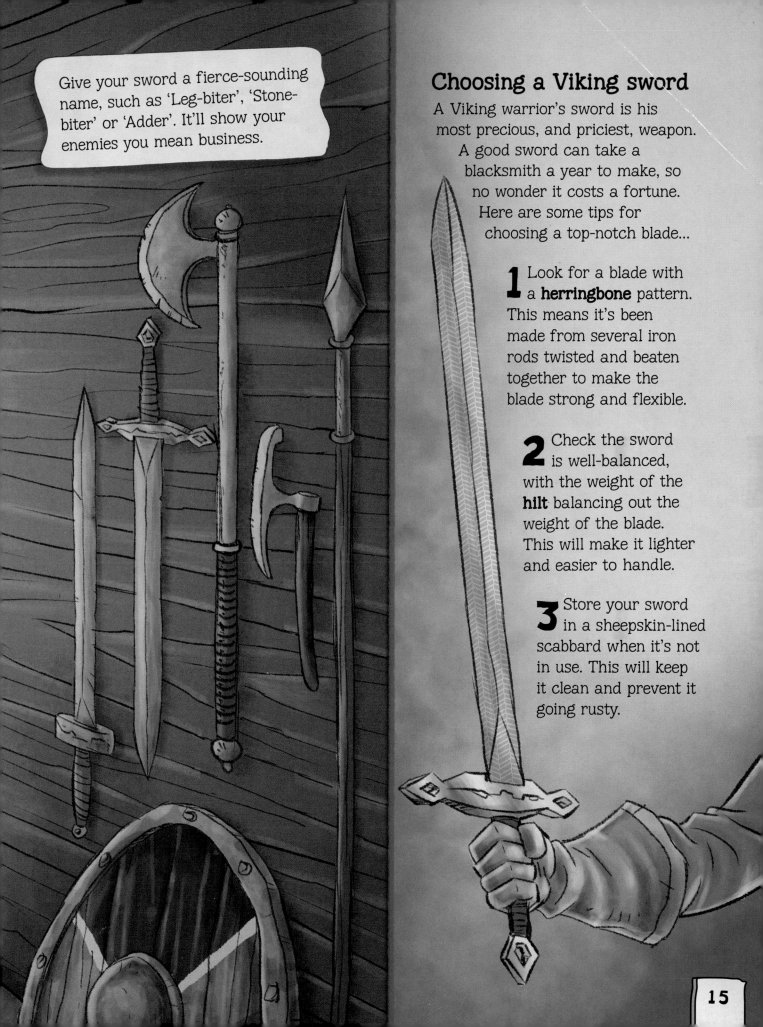

Give your sword a fierce-sounding name, such as 'Leg-biter', 'Stone-biter' or 'Adder'. It'll show your enemies you mean business.

Choosing a Viking sword

A Viking warrior's sword is his most precious, and priciest, weapon. A good sword can take a blacksmith a year to make, so no wonder it costs a fortune. Here are some tips for choosing a top-notch blade...

1 Look for a blade with a **herringbone** pattern. This means it's been made from several iron rods twisted and beaten together to make the blade strong and flexible.

2 Check the sword is well-balanced, with the weight of the **hilt** balancing out the weight of the blade. This will make it lighter and easier to handle.

3 Store your sword in a sheepskin-lined scabbard when it's not in use. This will keep it clean and prevent it going rusty.

15

Viking Warship

Any Viking raiding party worth its salt needs a longship, and we've spent weeks building a new one. It's going to be the best ever: lightning fast, strong and shallow enough to sail up rivers and land on beaches when we want to launch a surprise attack. It's made of finest oak and pine – only the best for my Dad – and it's around 22 metres (72 feet 3 inches) long. When it's finished, it'll have a dragon's head carved on the prow at the front. I've been practising rowing in case I need to take my turn at the oars, but there's also a sail for when the wind gets up.

How to build a longship

First, cut down an oak tree to make the **keel**. Then cut long planks of wood for the sides, and shorter planks for the cross-beams and ribs. Each side plank overlaps the one below to make the ship very strong. Join the pieces together with wooden pegs and iron nails, and stuff any cracks with sheeps' wool, dipped in tar, to make the ship watertight.

Tips for navigation

With no fancy instruments to help you navigate, you have to use your knowledge of the sun, moon, stars, waves and local landmarks to help you stay on course. Luckily, this is something you're very skilled at.

1 Sail as close to the coast as possible, looking out for landmarks on the shore.

2 During the day, use your sun compass (left, it's like a sundial). The higher the sun, the shorter is the shadow cast and the further south you are. The lower the sun, the further north you are.

3 At night, watch the stars. The Pole Star always points to the north.

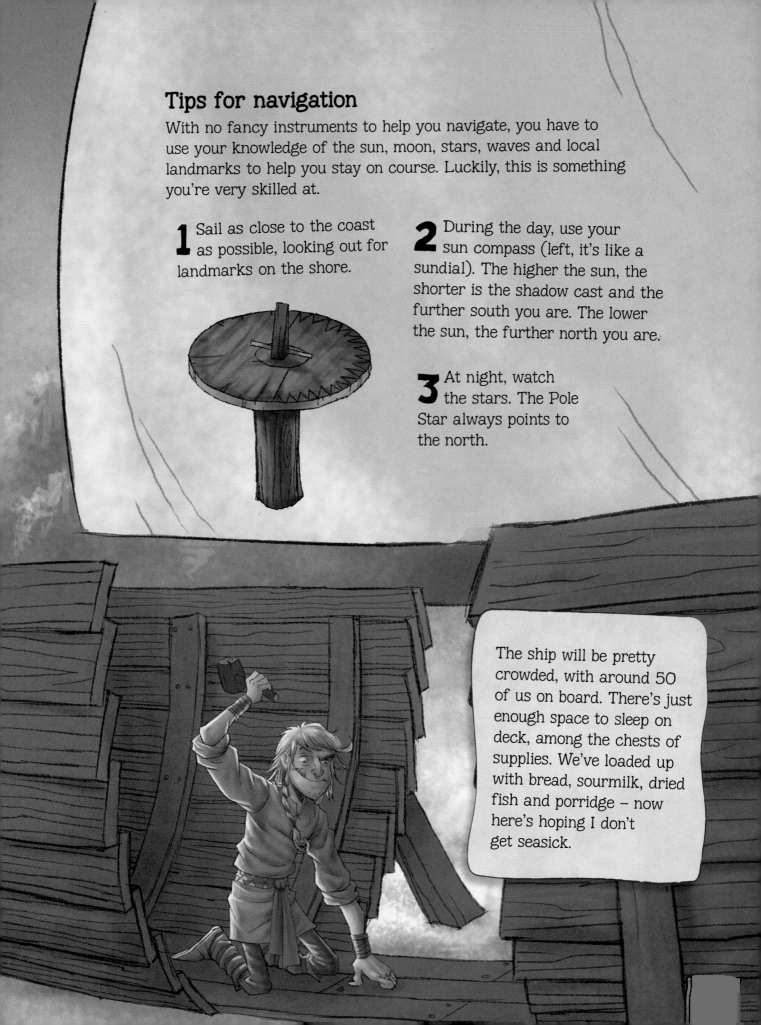

The ship will be pretty crowded, with around 50 of us on board. There's just enough space to sleep on deck, among the chests of supplies. We've loaded up with bread, sourmilk, dried fish and porridge – now here's hoping I don't get seasick.

A-Viking!

(Bjorn's first raid)

Wish I'd never mentioned the seasick bit. It has been terrible. We set off at dawn the day before last, and headed west. At first, the weather was good for sailing, with clear skies and a strong wind behind us. In fact, it was really boring, with nothing to do but eat, sleep and fish. Then a storm blew up…

Anyway, we finally reached north-east England where we're going to attack a monastery. My first raid is about to start, I'm going a-Viking! We must get in and out with our loot and prisoners as quickly as we can, and make my father proud.

The best time to go raiding is between April and October. After that, the weather gets horribly unsettled and you're at risk of being shipwrecked.

Norway

Sweden

England

Denmark

How to launch a raid

You're within sight of land and you're armed and ready to raid. Luckily, it's foggy so no one's spotted you, giving you the crucial element of surprise.

1 Run the ship ashore, jump out and haul it on to the beach.

2 Send an advance party ahead to cover any escape routes.

3 The rest of you attack the monastery. You need to be quick before the monks can send for help.

4 Grab as much treasure as you can, and take some of the monks prisoner.

5 Set fire to the monastery before heading back to the ship.

spoils of War

The raid's over and we're heading for home before the villagers come after us. We've been busy loading the ships with plunder. We took some of the monks prisoner – they'll be sold as slaves when we get back home. We picked the youngest and healthiest, so hopefully we'll get a good price for them. We also grabbed loads of gold and silver cups and coins, as well as boxes covered in jewels that held books and holy **relics**. My father says all this loot will be shared out among the raiders, with him getting the biggest helping, of course!

Some Vikings bury their loot for safety, always intending to come back later and reclaim their valuables. If they never make it, rich troves of treasure may be found in future, buried in farmers' fields. Imagine digging up that lot!

How to ransom a hostage

Choose the most important monks to **ransom**. Someone senior like an abbot can fetch a fortune.

1 Put a handsome price on your hostage. Remember, gold is worth much more than silver.

2 Promise the ransom-payer safe passage; you don't want to put them off before you get the cash.

3 Look after any hostages well, unless the ransom isn't paid. Then you can choose to sell them as slaves.

4 You can also hold holy objects, books and relics to ransom. People will pay well to get these treasures back.

WARNING!

Guard your prisoners carefully. If they escape, you can wave goodbye to your profits!

Victory Feast

WARNING!

Don't eat too much at the feast or you might end up breaking your bench!

We're safely back home, and my father's throwing a huge feast to celebrate a successful raid. It's a chance for him to show off how rich (and generous) he is, so there's plenty of food and drink. I'm tucking into my third helping of boiled blood pudding – delicious. Everyone's wearing their best clothes and jewellery, and has crammed into the hall. The feast will go on for hours yet, so I might slip off to bed, before the boasting begins…

Boasting about how brave and strong you are is an important part of any Viking feast. But don't fall into the trap of boasting about something you can't do. If you show off about taking on the enemy single-handed, make sure you can live up to it: your honour is at stake.

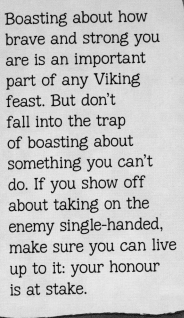

Writing a poem

The skald (poet) has composed a poem about my father's latest victory. It'd better be good. Here's some top tips for writing your own.

1 Go on a raid yourself, then you'll know what you're talking about.

2 Big up the jarl's achievements – your job is to make him look good.

3 Use lots of fancy turns of phrase, like 'weapon storm' for battle and 'battle sweat' for blood.

Bitter Battle

A year has passed since my first raid, and now we're back in Britain, in the far north of Scotland. This time there are a few hundred of us and a fleet of longships. We've come over to fight the Scots and grab some land. My father says he doesn't have enough to give all his sons a decent plot, so he wants to take some from the Scots. But the Scots are fighting back bravely and, at the moment, we're surrounded. The plan is to form a guard around my Dad, using our shields to make a wall. If he's killed, we're in trouble.

Start looking and sounding like a winner, even before you go into battle. It'll scare your enemy (you hope). Polish your weapons and armour, and make as much noise as you can. Don't forget to pray to Odin, god of war – it might not help but it can't do any harm.

How to fight like a berserker

If you really want to make your mark in battle, become a berserker, the wildest Viking warrior of all. Here's what to do:

1 Before battle, work yourself up into a frenzy, howling and biting on your shield.

2 Don't bother with armour. Wear a scary bearskin or wolfskin instead.

3 Fly into a fury as you fight: worrying about being killed is for wimps.

WARNING!

Bad luck if you're picked as **standard bearer.** You won't be able to defend yourself so you'll make an easy target for the enemy.

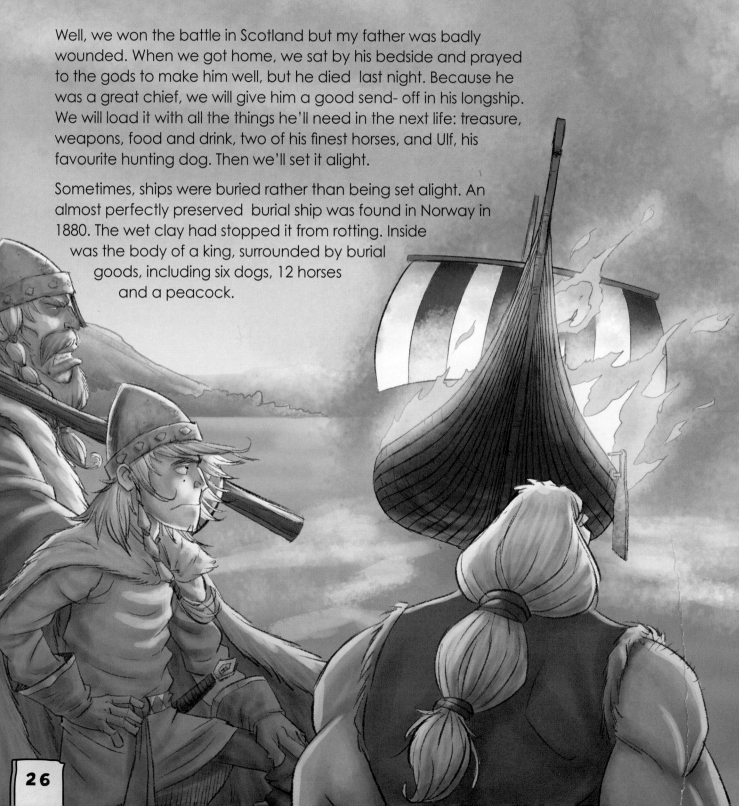

Death of a Warrior

Well, we won the battle in Scotland but my father was badly wounded. When we got home, we sat by his bedside and prayed to the gods to make him well, but he died last night. Because he was a great chief, we will give him a good send- off in his longship. We will load it with all the things he'll need in the next life: treasure, weapons, food and drink, two of his finest horses, and Ulf, his favourite hunting dog. Then we'll set it alight.

Sometimes, ships were buried rather than being set alight. An almost perfectly preserved burial ship was found in Norway in 1880. The wet clay had stopped it from rotting. Inside was the body of a king, surrounded by burial goods, including six dogs, 12 horses and a peacock.

How to bury a chief

Only the richest and most important Vikings are given a ship burial. Here's how to make sure things run smoothly.

1 Dress the chief in his best clothes and finest jewellery.

2 Place his body in a tent on the deck of his longship.

3 Pack all of his belongings around him.

4 Set the ship on fire as it floats away.

Most Vikings can't afford a longship. If you're lucky, you might be buried in a small rowing boat or in a grave marked out by stones in a longship shape. That's as close as you'll get to the real thing.

Gods of War

It's been a sad time since my father's death, but at least we know that he died a hero. That's the greatest honour for a Viking warrior and means that he'll join the band of warriors at Valhalla, Odin's hall in Asgard (the realm of the gods). There the warriors spend their days practising their fighting skills, and their nights feasting on the finest food and drink. Bet my Dad will enjoy that!

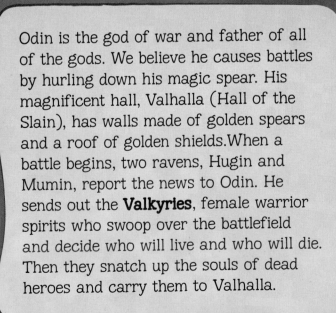

Odin is the god of war and father of all of the gods. We believe he causes battles by hurling down his magic spear. His magnificent hall, Valhalla (Hall of the Slain), has walls made of golden spears and a roof of golden shields. When a battle begins, two ravens, Hugin and Mumin, report the news to Odin. He sends out the **Valkyries**, female warrior spirits who swoop over the battlefield and decide who will live and who will die. Then they snatch up the souls of dead heroes and carry them to Valhalla.

Ragnarok – the Last Battle

Vikings believe there will be a last great battle, called Ragnarok, which will cause the downfall of the gods and the end of the world. After Ragnarok, Midgard (the land of humans) will freeze over. All humans will be killed, apart from one couple. The sun and moon will be eaten by wolves, plunging the world into darkness and chaos. Eventually, a new world will rise up, with a new race of gods and people. Hopefully!

Ten Vicious Viking Facts

1 The Vikings definitely lived up to their name. The word 'Viking' means 'pirate raid'.

2 Vikings fed injured warriors onion soup, then smelled them to see how bad their wounds were.

3 Viking bread was made from flour, water and so much grit that it wore their teeth down.

4 If you killed another Viking, you had to pay *wergild* or 'blood money' to his family.

5 'Never leave your weapons behind when you go to the fields; you may need them. (Viking saying)

6 A Viking's toilet was a hole in the ground, with moss or sheep's wool for toilet paper.

7 Viking leader, Ivan the Boneless, may have got his name from having such weak legs that his men carried him into battle on a shield.

8 Viking warriors were afraid to die in bed in case they went to Niflheim, the Underworld.

9 Viking nicknames included 'Troll-burster', 'Squint-eyed', 'Bent backwards' and 'Foul fart'.

10 Erik the Red, who discovered Greenland, gave it its fine-sounding name to encourage more Vikings to go there.

Glossary

Byrnie
A shirt made from mail

Herringbone
A pattern made from V-shapes

Hilt
The handle of a sword

Hird
A group of warriors who fought for a jarl

Jarl
A wealthy noble, or earl, in Viking society

Keel
The long piece of wood that runs from one end of a ship to the other along the base, supporting the whole structure

Oath
A solemn and binding promise

Ransom
Money paid for the safe return of a prisoner or precious object

Relic
A holy object, such as the bones or belongings of a saint

Skald
A Viking poet

Standard bearer
Someone who carries a standard (army's flag) into battle

Valkyries
Odin's handmaidens, who carried the souls of dead warriors to Valhalla

INDEX

The Author
Anita Ganeri is an award-winning author of educational children's books. She has written on a huge variety of subjects, from Vikings to viruses and from Romans to world religions. She was born in India but now lives in England with her family and pets.

The Artist
Mariano Epelbaum was born in Buenos Aires, Argentina. He grew up drawing and looking at small insects under the stones in the garden of his grandmother´s house. He has worked as an art director and character designer for many films in Argentina and Spain.